Super Cute Things to Draw

Everything Cute

Lauren Bergstrom

Walter Foster

Quarto.com

This library edition published in 2024 by Walter Foster Publishing,
an imprint of The Quarto Group.

100 Cummings Center, Suite 265-D, Beverly, MA 01915, USA.
T (978) 282-9590 F (978) 283-2742

Distributed in the United States and Canada
by Lerner Publisher Services
241 First Avenue North
Minneapolis, MN 55401 U.S.A.
www.lernerbooks.com

First Library Edition

Library of Congress Cataloging-in-Publication Data

Names: Bergstrom, Lauren, author.
Title: Super cute things to draw : everything cute / Lauren Bergstrom.
Other titles: Everything cute
Description: First library edition. | Beverly, MA, USA : Walter Foster Publishing, an imprint of The Quarto Group, 2022. | "Step-by-step lessons for making super cute drawings in a super simple way!"--Cover. | Audience: Ages 8-12 | Audience: Grades 4-6 | Summary: "Everything Cute includes step-by-step drawing projects for beginning artists-with adorable animals, cuddly critters, and fantasy creatures"-- Provided by publisher.
Identifiers: LCCN 2024003406 | ISBN 9780760391204 (hardcover)
Subjects: LCSH: Drawing--Technique--Juvenile literature. | Cartooning--Technique--Juvenile literature.
Classification: LCC NC655 .B48 2022 | DDC 741.2--dc23/eng20240305
LC record available at https://lccn.loc.gov/2024003406

Printed in USA
10 9 8 7 6 5 4 3 2 1

Table of Contents

INTRODUCTION

Create your very own little kawaii world with ***Super Cute Things to Draw!*** Take a walk in a tiny forest of your own creation, or fly among rainbows, clouds, and shooting stars. Meet creatures both real and imagined, but all brimming with cuteness and personality.

Doodling can be a fun and relaxing activity for all ages, and this book will show you how. There are drawing lessons for 50 adorable things to inspire your imagination. Use these projects as a starting point for your own creativity, and don't worry about being perfect. Just have fun and let your own style shine through!

TOOLS & MATERIALS

You don't need anything special to start drawing. Choose supplies that you're comfortable with and enjoy using. Here are some suggestions to get you started:

Paper
Notebooks and sketchbooks are great for taking your doodles anywhere you go. If you're using markers, choose thicker paper so that the colors don't bleed through.

Gel Pens
Gel pens can be used to draw outlines and fill in small areas of color. They come in many colors, including neon, white, and metallic, which can be used to add highlights and sparkles.

Colored Pencils
Use these to color in your drawings. You can layer different colors to make them more interesting. Good quality colored pencils have a smooth feel, and will create more vibrant colors.

Fineliner Pens
Fineliner pens with pigment ink have very fine tips, and are good for drawing thin outlines and little details.

Brush Markers
Brush markers have a soft tip that looks a bit like a paintbrush. They can be used to add color to your drawings, and you can blend different colors together to make interesting effects.

DRAWING TIPS & TECHNIQUES

Everybody has their own unique drawing style, so feel free to experiment and try different things. You can even draw the same thing in different ways to see which one you like best. Here are some different things you could try:

Using Different Outlines

You don't have to be limited to using black for outlines. Try brown, blue, red, or green instead. You can also experiment with thicker or thinner outlines to see which you prefer.

Mixing Materials & Tools

Try adding colored pencil shading on top of brush markers (like the octopus on the left) or gel pen details on top of colored pencil (like the octopus on the right). Different materials can create very different effects!

Adding Paint
Watercolor and gouache paints can be used to fill in larger areas of color, or to add details. Gouache is particularly good for adding lighter details on top of a darker color.

Experimenting with Faces
Faces add character and personality to your drawings, so play around with different facial expressions. Here is a chart with many different faces to try!

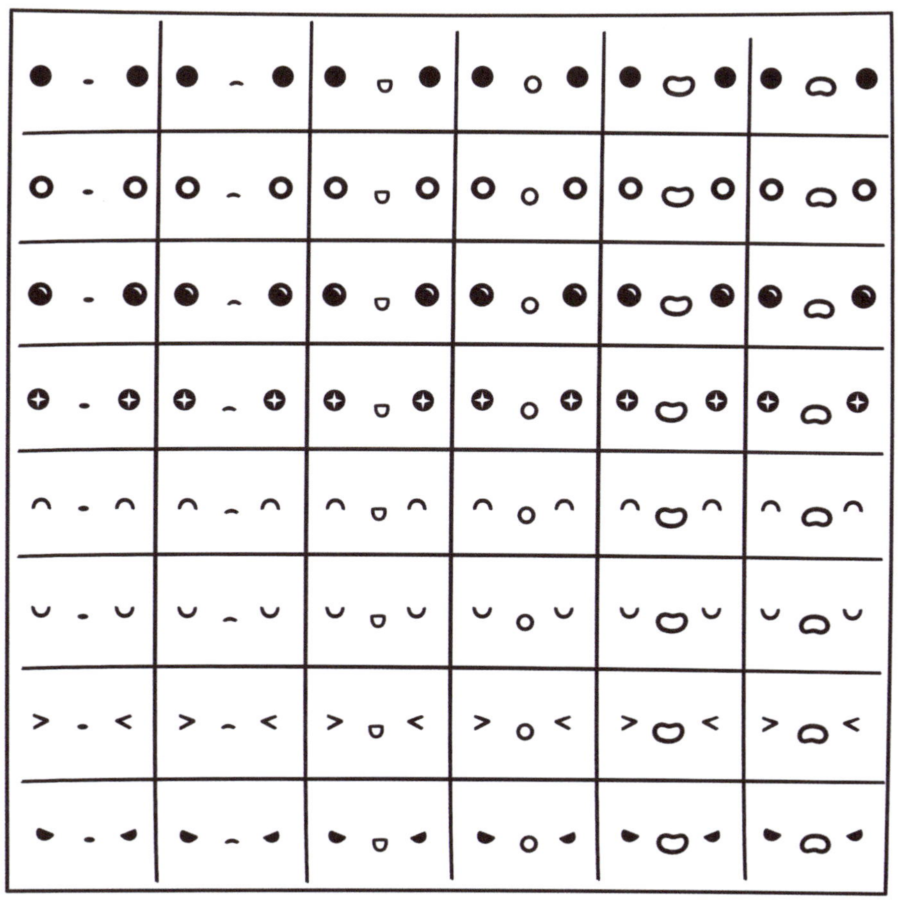

USING COLOR

The color wheel is a visual way to show basic color theory. Understanding the relationships between colors will help you choose which colors to use to bring your drawings to life.

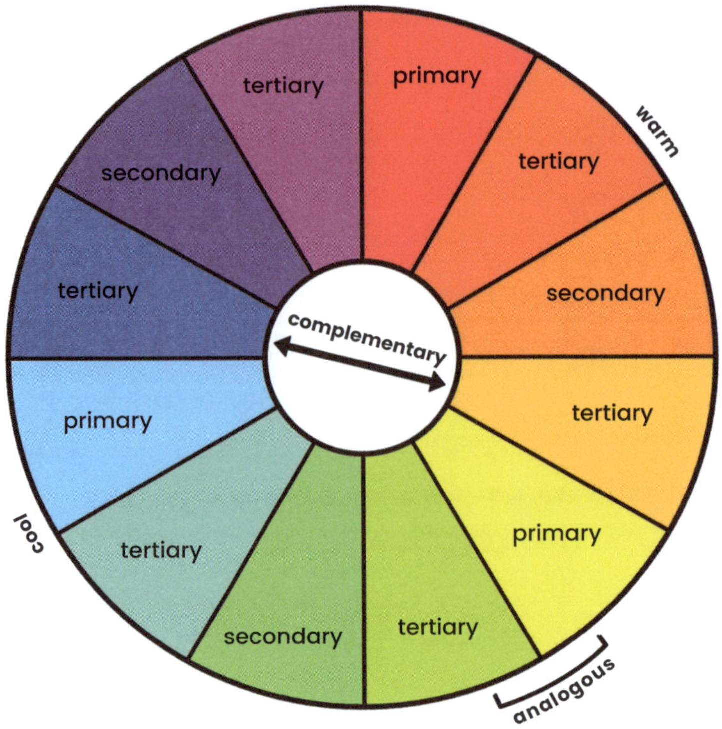

Primary Colors
Red, yellow, and blue are primary colors. They can't be created by mixing other colors.

Secondary Colors
Orange, green, and purple are secondary colors. They are made by mixing two primary colors together.

Tertiary Colors
Mix a primary and a secondary color together and you have a tertiary color! These include red-orange, yellow-orange, yellow-green, blue-green, blue-purple, and red-purple.

Color Temperature
Red, orange, and yellow are "warm" colors. Blue, green, and purple are "cool" colors.

Complementary Colors
Colors directly across from each other on the color wheel are called complementary colors, such as red and green or orange and blue. These colors make each other stand out, and look bright and bold together.

Analogous Colors
Colors next to each other on the color wheel are called analogous colors, such as green and blue-green, or yellow and yellow-green. These colors look harmonious together and can be used to create gradients of color.

CREATING TEXTURES & PATTERNS

You can use textures and patterns to make your drawings more interesting. Try experimenting with different kinds of marks and strokes. Here are some examples to get you started.

Hatching

Make lots of lines in the same direction. The lines can be long or short, close together or far apart.

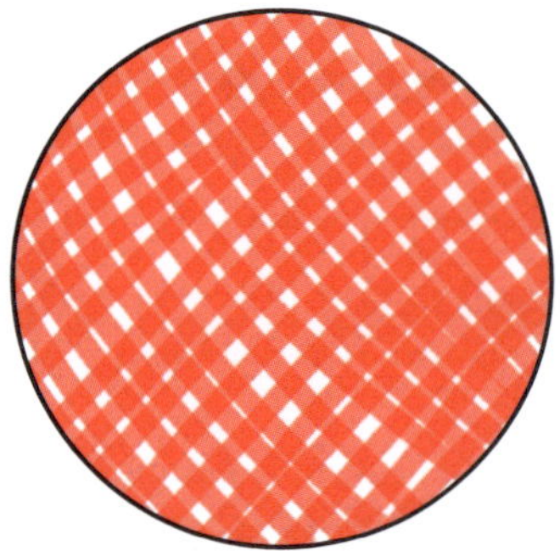

Crosshatching

Make lots of lines in opposite directions. Like hatching, the lines can be long or short, close together or far apart.

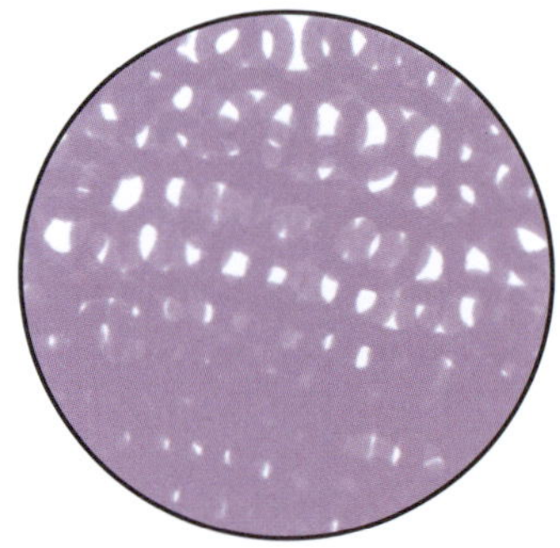

Scumbling

Fill in areas of color by scribbling in a small, circular motion. Denser scribbles will create darker colors.

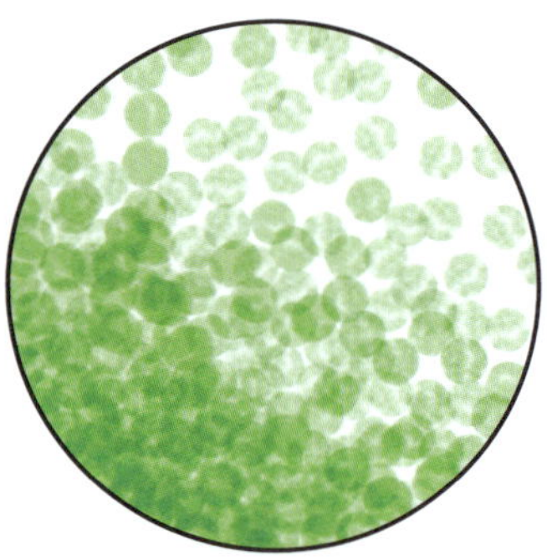

Stippling

Fill in an area with lots of little dots. Make the dots closer together for darker areas.

Gradating

Shade an area from dark to light by adding more layers of color to the darker area.

Blending

Blend two colors together by making two gradated areas that overlap in the middle.

There are endless possibilities when it comes to adding cute patterns. Here are a few ideas.

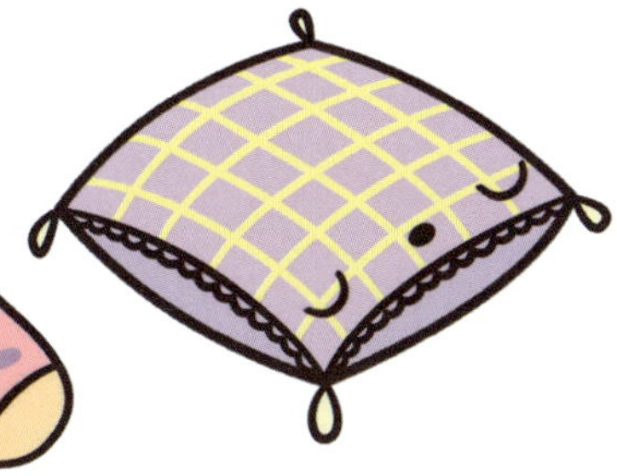

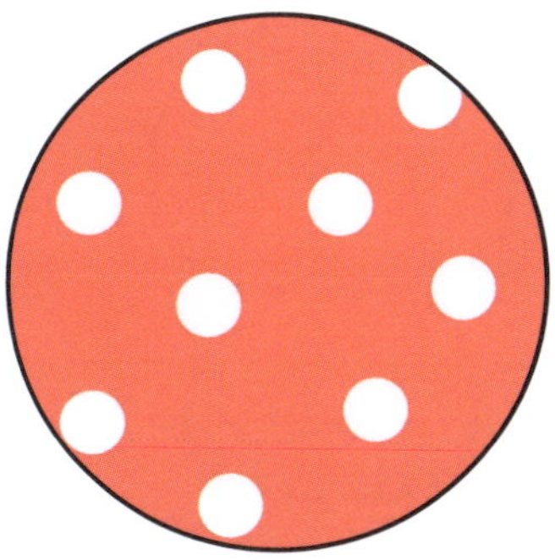

Polka dots

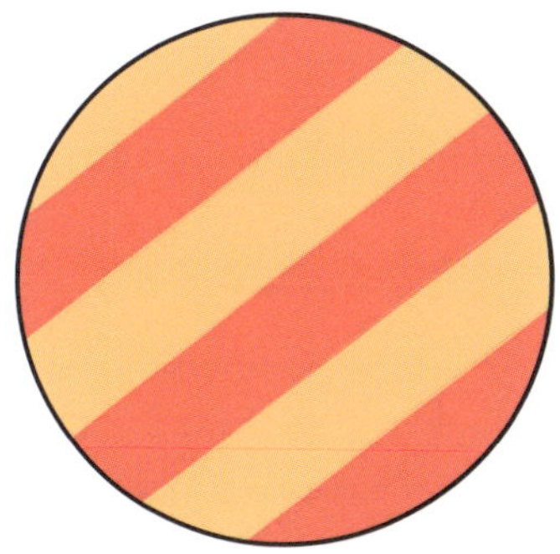

Thick stripes

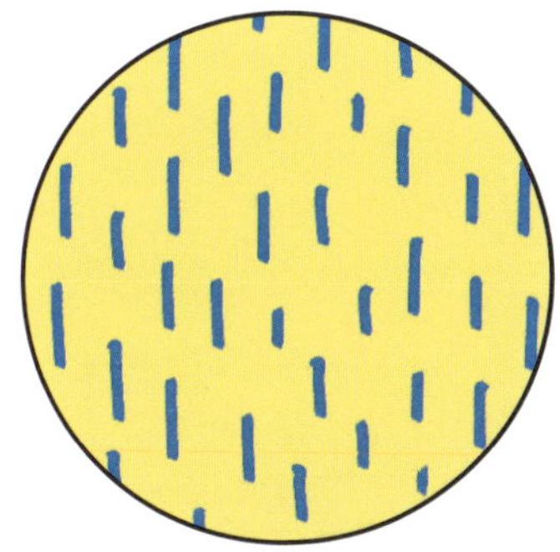

Raindrops

Checkers

Flowers

Wavy lines

Thin stripes

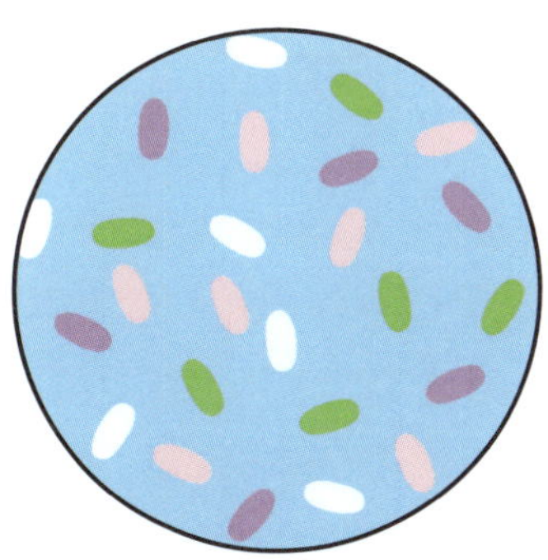

Sprinkles

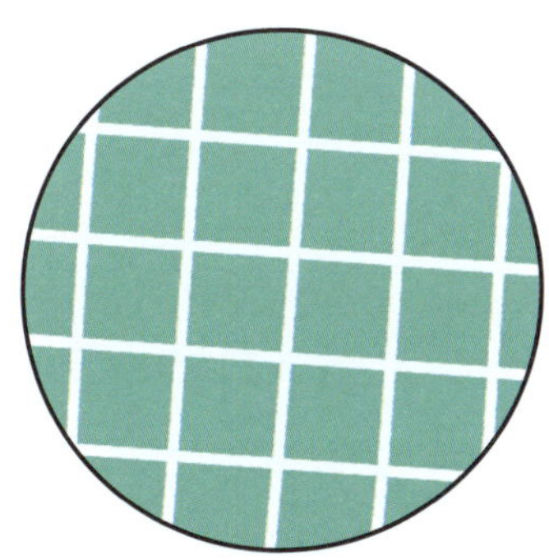

Grid

Fox

1. Start with a blob-shaped head and a small body.

2. Draw a curved line for the tail, with another line near the tip of the tail.

3. Add two legs onto the front of the body.

4. Draw two triangle-shaped ears on top of the head.

5. Draw a curved line in the middle of the head. Then add two eyes and a nose.

6. Color in your fox! Use white for the face and dark brown for the paws and ears.

Squirrel

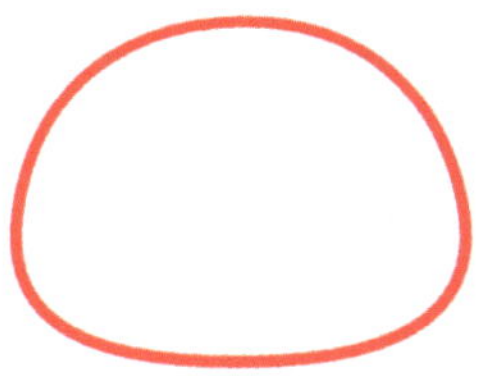

1. Start by drawing a blob-shaped head.

2. Draw a small body under the head.

3. Give the squirrel a big tail with a curved tip.

4. Add some ears, hands, and feet.

5. Draw a cute face onto the squirrel's head.

6. Color in your squirrel, giving it a lighter-colored tummy and some pink blush under the eyes.

Raccoon

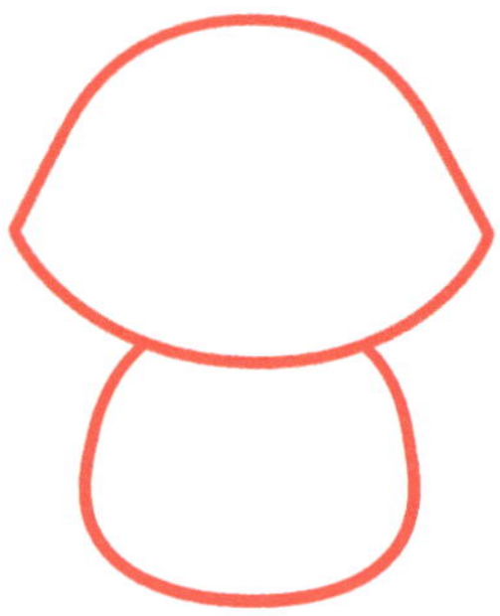

1. Start by drawing a small body and a head with slightly pointy sides.

2. Draw the mask shape in the middle of the head.

3. Add two big eyes and a tiny mouth and nose.

4. Draw a tail with some curved lines for stripes.

5. Give the raccoon some ears, arms, and feet.

6. Color in your raccoon, adding a dark mask and stripes but a lighter-colored tummy.

Bear

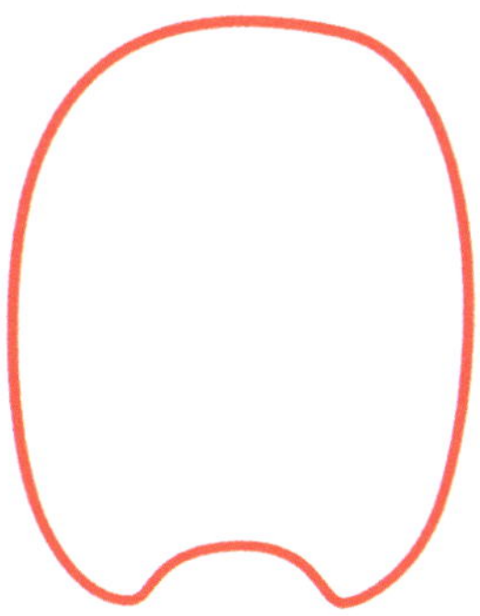

1. Start by drawing the bear's body shape.

2. Add two eyes and a snout with a small nose.

3. Draw two rounded ears on top of the head.

4. Give the bear two little arms.

5. Draw a tummy on the front of the bear.

6. Color your bear brown, but use a lighter color for the tummy, snout, and ears.

Llama

1. Start by drawing a tall fluffy body shape.

2. Draw a face with a fluffy top and rounded bottom.

3. Add two circle eyes and a small nose.

4. Draw two ears on top of the head and two feet on the bottom.

5. Give the llama a cute pom-pom collar.

6. Color in your llama.

Red Panda

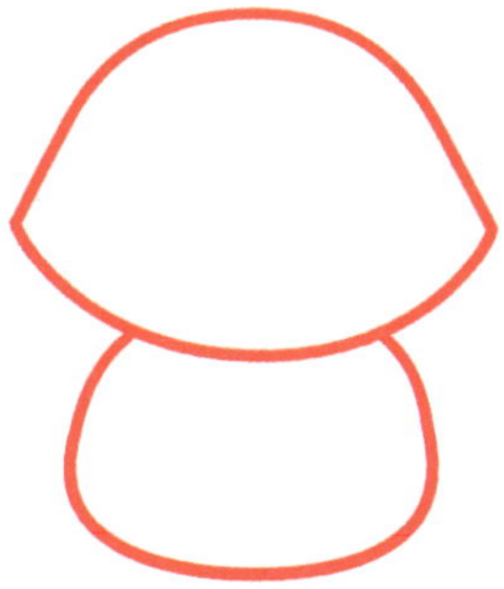

1. Start by drawing a small body and a head with slightly pointy sides.

2. Draw a snout with a small mouth and nose.

3. Add two eyes, eyebrows, and cheek marks.

4. Draw two ears, two arms, and two feet.

5. Add a tail with some curved lines for the stripes.

6. Color in your red panda, using a darker color for the tummy, inner ears, paws, and tail stripes.

Giant Panda

1. Start by drawing a chubby body shaped a bit like an egg.

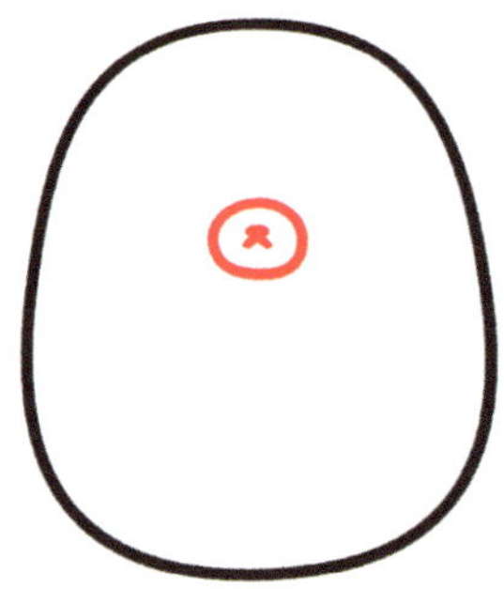

2. Add a small snout with a tiny mouth and nose.

3. Draw two eyes and add an oval shape around each.

4. Draw two ears, two arms, and two feet.

5. Add two curved lines over the midsection.

6. Color in your giant panda, using a darker color for the ears, eyes, feet, and the stripe over the tummy.

Sloth

1. Start by drawing a chubby body shaped a bit like an egg.

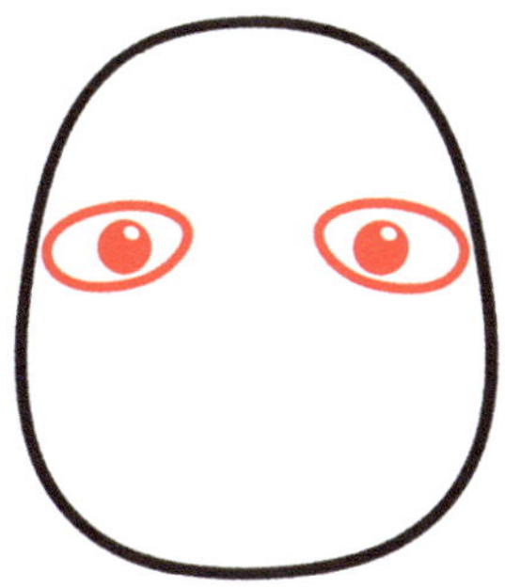

2. Draw two eyes. Then add a thin oval shape around each eye.

3. Add a small mouth and nose in between the eyes.

4. Give the sloth two long arms.

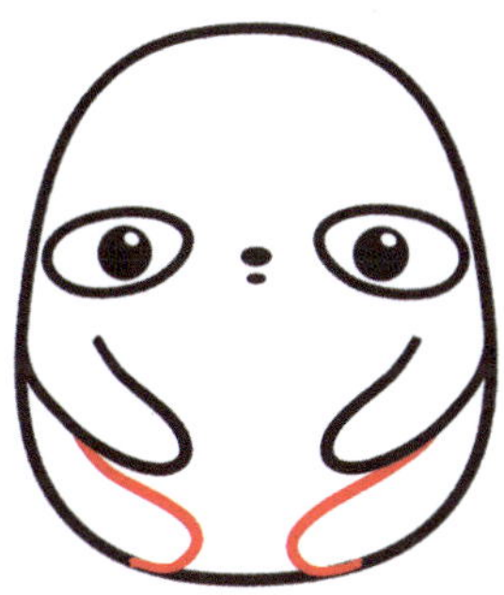

5. Add two long legs underneath the arms.

6. Color in your sloth, using a darker color around the eyes and a lighter color on the tummy.

Giraffe

1. Start by drawing a small egg-shaped head.

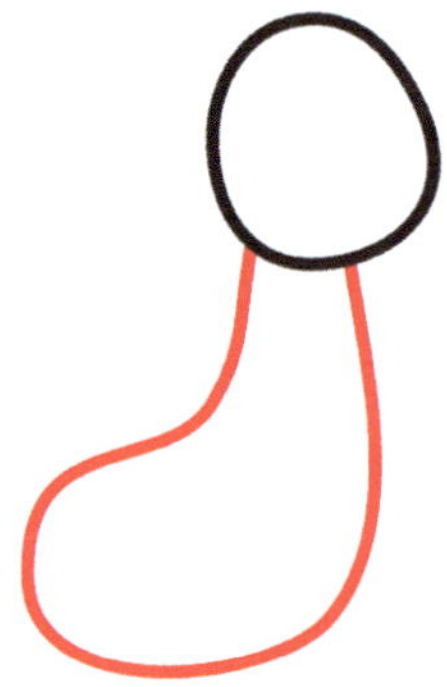

2. Add a body with a long neck.

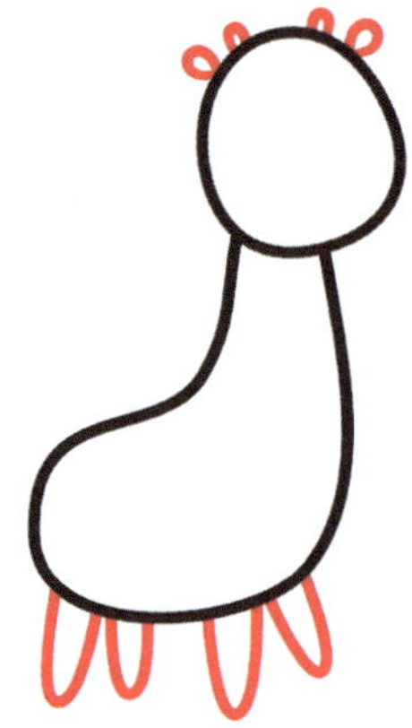

3. Draw four legs, as well as small ears and horns on top of the head.

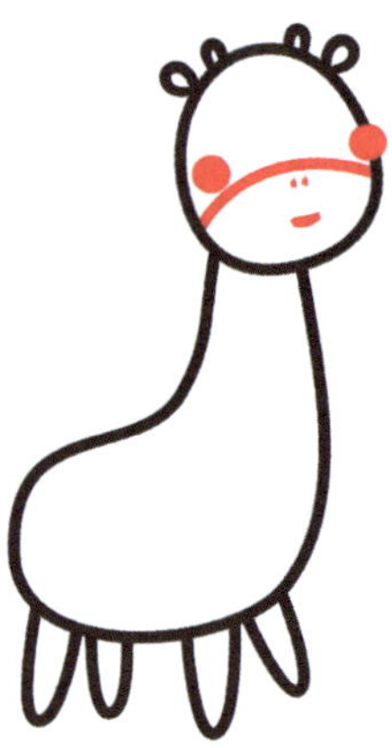

4. Add a curved line for the snout. Then draw the eyes, nostrils, and mouth.

5. Give the giraffe a tiny tail and some large patches on the body.

6. Color in your giraffe, using yellow for the body and dark brown for the spots.

Lion

1. Start by drawing a blob-shaped head with a big fluffy mane.

2. Add a snout, nose, mouth, and eyes.

3. Draw two small front legs under the mane.

4. Add two back legs and a curved line to complete the body.

5. Give the lion two ears and a tail with a fluffy tip.

6. Color in your lion, using a darker color for the mane and tip of the tail.

Koala

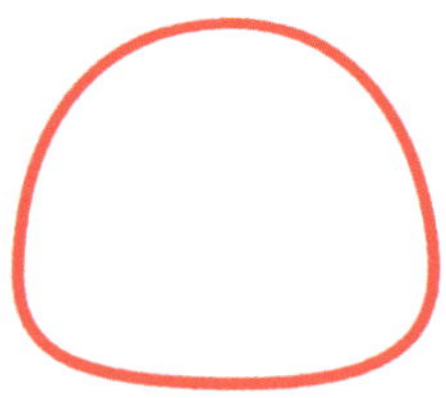

1. Start by drawing a gumdrop-shaped head.

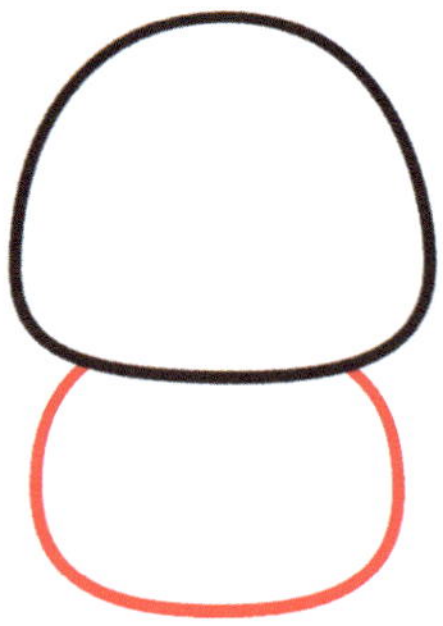

2. Add a round, chubby body under the head.

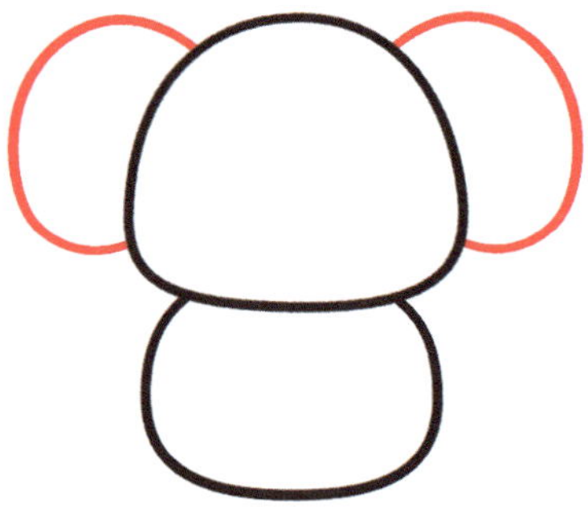

3. Draw a big ear on each side of the head.

4. Give the koala two long arms and two round feet.

5. Add two eyes, a big nose, and a tiny mouth.

6. Color in your koala with gray, adding a lighter-colored tummy and pink details.

Sheep

1. Start by drawing a fluffy cloud shape.

2. Add a face that's rounded at the bottom and fluffy on top.

3. Draw two eyes and a small nose.

4. Add two ears at the top corners of the face.

5. Draw some hooves underneath the body.

6. Color in your sheep!

Cow

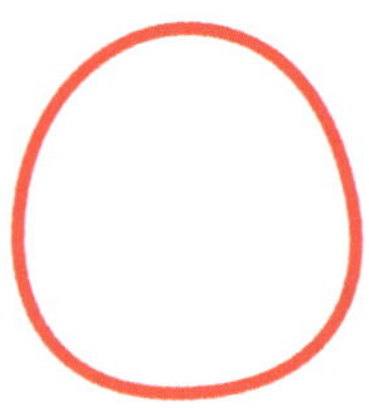

1. Start by drawing a big head shaped a bit like an egg.

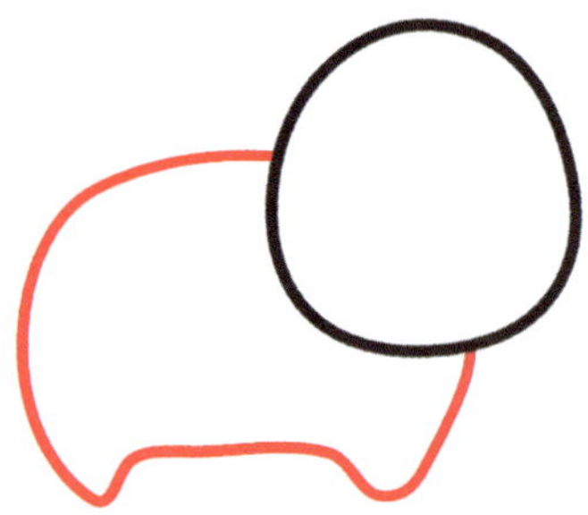

2. Add a chubby body with short legs.

3. Draw a curved line for the snout, and add two oval nostrils.

4. Add the eyes, horns, and ears.

5. Give the cow some spots and a little tail.

6. Color in your cow, using a darker color for the spots, horns, and tail tip.

Bunny

1. Start by drawing a round head with two long ears.

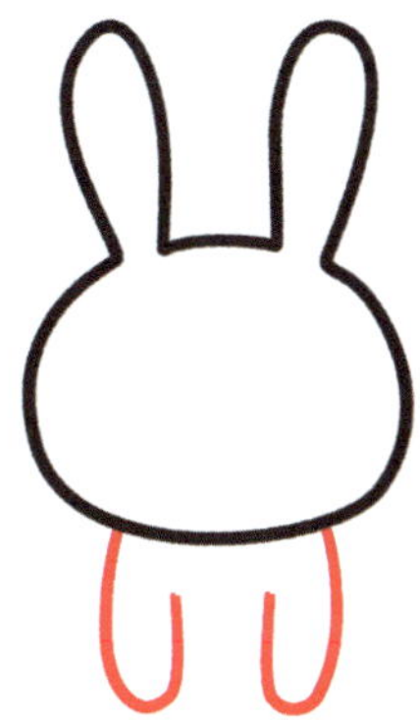

2. Draw two long front legs under the head.

3. Add two back legs. Then draw a curved line along the bottom to complete the body.

4. Give the bunny two big eyes and a small nose.

5. Draw two smaller ear shapes inside the ears.

6. Color in your bunny, using a light pink for the tummy and blush under the eyes.

Bird

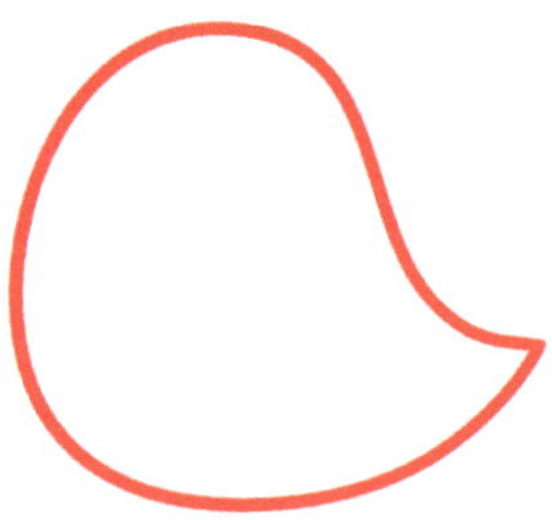

1. Start by drawing a chubby body shape that comes to a point on the right side.

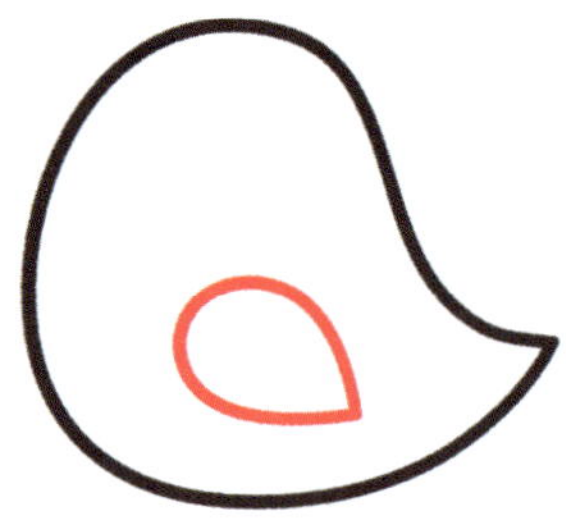

2. Add a small wing with a pointy tip.

3. Draw a big eye and a tiny beak.

4. Add two little legs and a crown shape on top of the head.

5. Draw some little lines for feathers on the tummy.

6. Color in your bird using whatever color you'd like.

Hedgehog

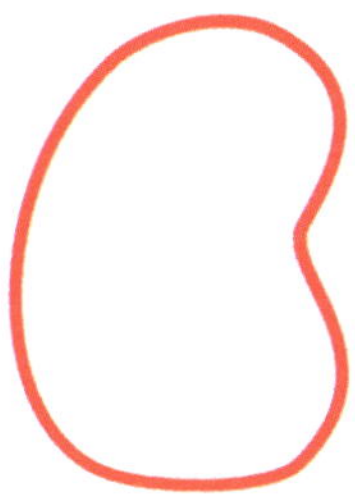

1. Start by drawing a small bean-shaped body.

2. Add two eyes and a nose.

3. Draw two tiny arms and two little legs.

4. Add the spiky spines on the hedgehog's back.

5. Draw two tiny ears on top of the head.

6. Color in your hedgehog with brown, using a lighter color on the tummy.

Guinea Pig

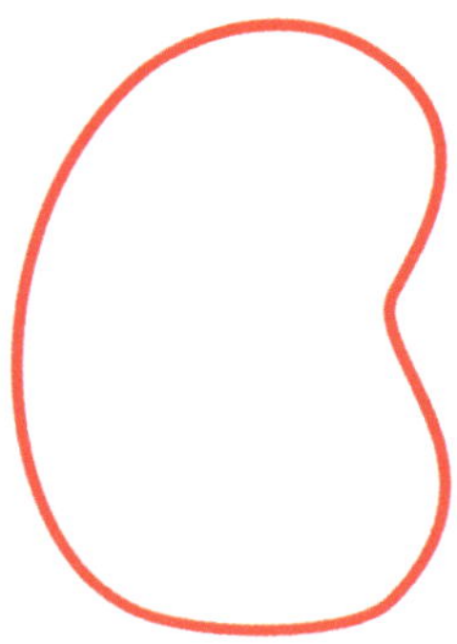

1. Start by drawing a bean-shaped body.

2. Add two big eyes and a nose.

3. Draw a curved line for a patch around one eye.

4. Add four little limbs.

5. Draw two triangular ears on top of the head.

6. Color in your guinea pig, using a darker color for the eye patch and ears.

Dog

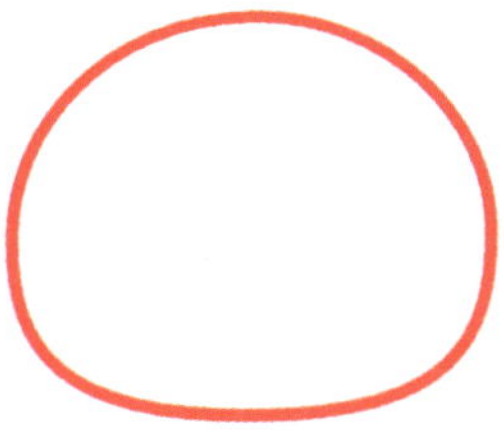

1. Start by drawing a big, round head.

2. Draw two front legs under the head.

3. Add two back legs and then a curved line to complete the body.

4. Draw a curved line in the middle of the head. Then add two eyes and a nose.

5. Add two triangular ears and oval eyebrows above the eyes.

6. Color in your dog with a Shiba Inu coloring, leaving the eyebrows, the insides of the ears, and the tummy white.

Cat

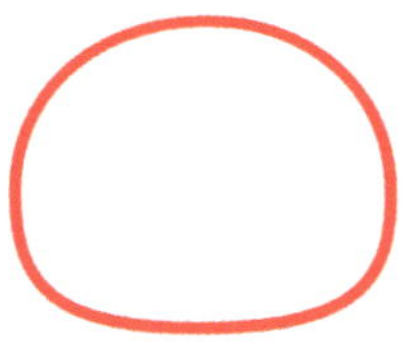

1. Start by drawing a slightly squashed circle for the head.

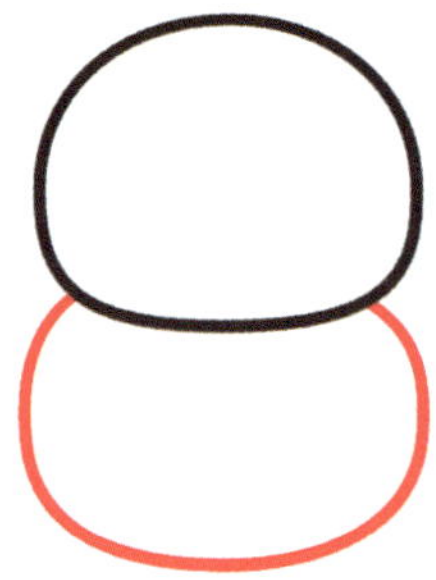

2. Draw a big, chubby body under the head.

3. Add two eyes, a nose, and whiskers.

4. Draw four little paws on the cat's body.

5. Add a long tail and two triangular ears.

6. Color in your cat, using a lighter color inside the ears and on the tummy.

Dumbo Octopus

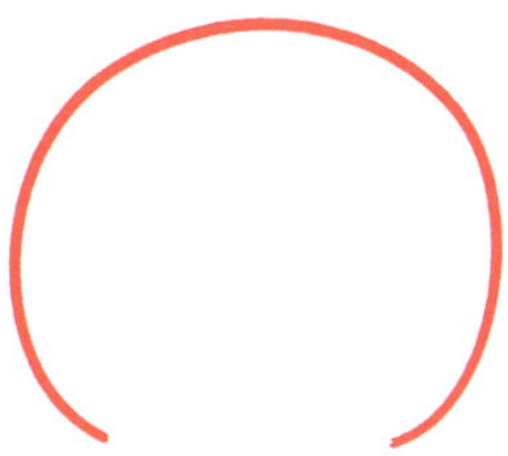

1. Start by drawing a circle with an open bottom.

2. Add tentacles under the circle with a wavy line.

3. Draw two big eyes and a little open mouth on the lower part of the body.

4. Add two floppy ears on top of the head.

5. Draw some little spots on the head.

6. Color in your dumbo octopus.

Whale

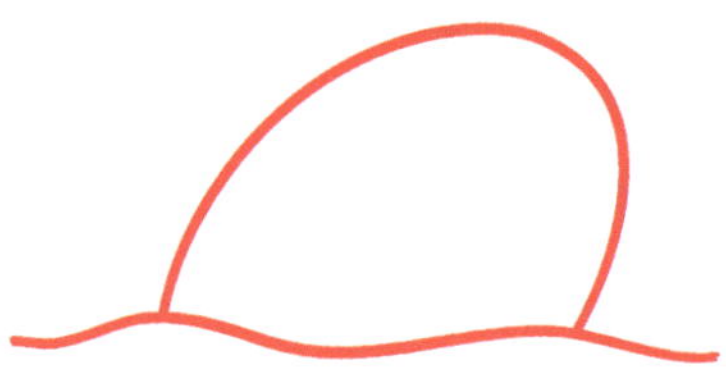

1. Start by drawing a wavy line with a big, curved line for the whale's body.

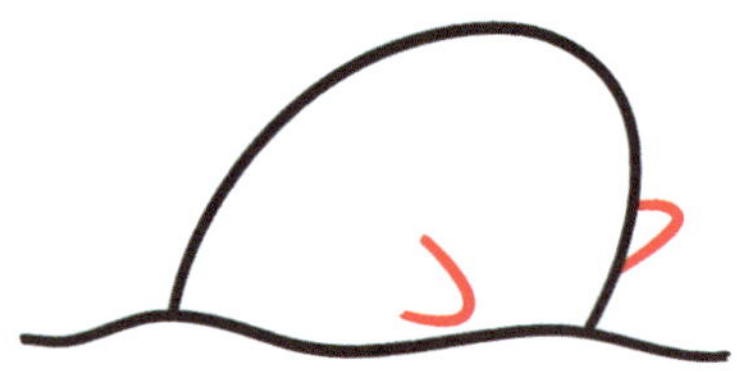

2. Draw two flippers on the body.

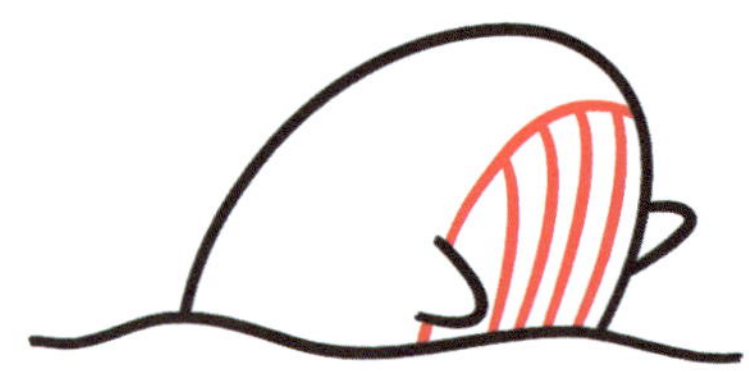

3. Add another curved line with some stripes along the tummy.

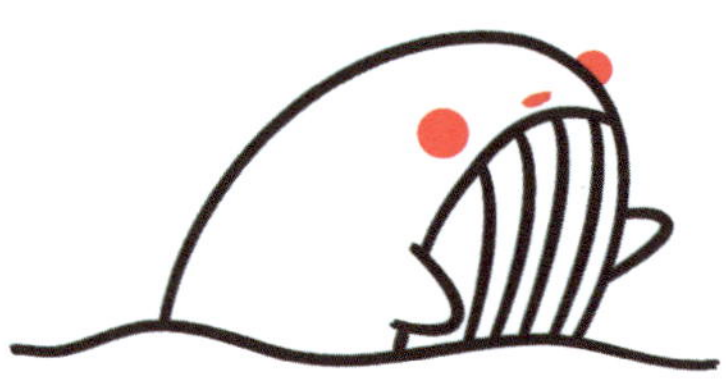

4. Draw two big eyes and a little mouth on the whale's head.

5. Add some water splashes coming out of your whale's blowhole near the top of the head.

6. Color in your whale!

Mermaid

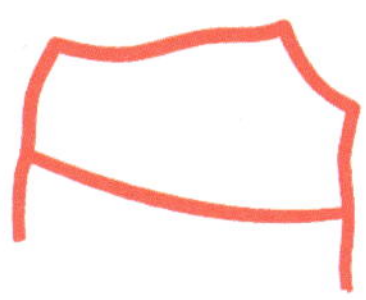

1. Start with a slightly curved line for the chin. Then add a hairline to frame the face.

2. Use a wavy line to create the rest of the hair. Draw a flower in the hair.

3. Draw two eyes and a little mouth on the face.

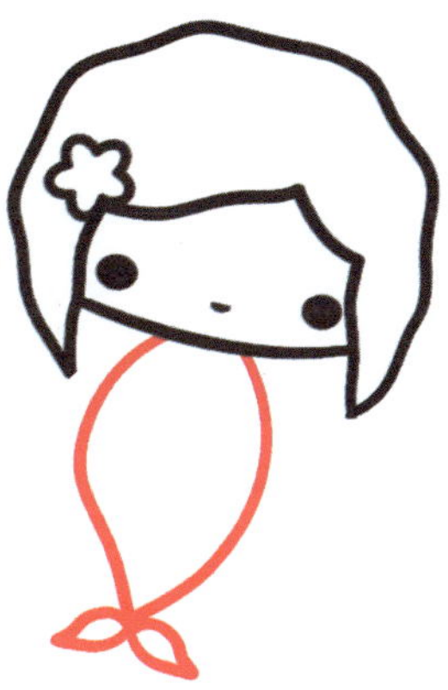

4. Draw the mermaid's body, with two fins at the tip of the tail.

5. Add two arms, a waist, and two curved lines for the mermaid's top.

6. Color in your mermaid, using color to add details on the tail.

Fairy

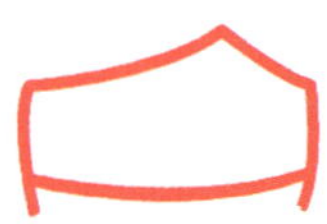

1. Start with a slightly curved line for the chin, and then add a hairline to frame the face.

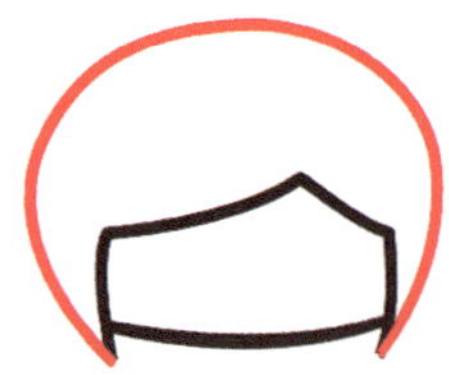

2. Draw a big, curved line for the rest of the head and hair.

3. Add two eyes and a mouth on the face, and two little circles for hair accessories.

4. Draw the fairy's outfit, with two little buttons at the top.

5. Give the fairy some little arms and legs, and big wings.

6. Color in your fairy, using white to add sparkles on the wings and hair.

Yeti

1. Start by drawing an oval body with some fur sticking up on the top.

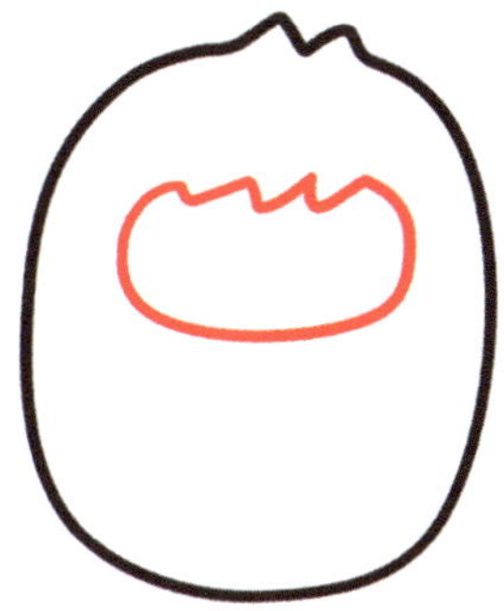

2. Draw a face with a rounded bottom and furry top.

3. Add two big eyes and a little mouth on the face.

4. Give the yeti two arms and two legs.

5. Draw two horns on top of the head and some fur on the chest.

6. Color in your yeti!

Dragon

1. Start by drawing a big head with a small, round body.

2. Add two eyes, a mouth, and some spikes on the head.

3. Draw two arms and two feet on the body.

4. Add a pointy tail with some spikes on top.

5. Give the dragon wings and fin-shaped ears.

6. Color in your dragon, using a lighter color for the tummy and darker lines on the wings and ears.

Griffin

1. Start by drawing a round head with a feathery bottom.

2. Draw two front legs with little claws at the ends.

3. Add the back legs and draw a curved line between the front legs to complete the body.

4. Draw two eyes, a beak, and two triangular ears.

5. Give the griffin two wings and a tail with a fluffy tip.

6. Color in your griffin!

Pegasus

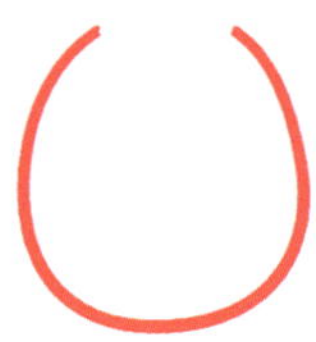

1. Start by drawing an oval head, leaving a gap at the top for the mane.

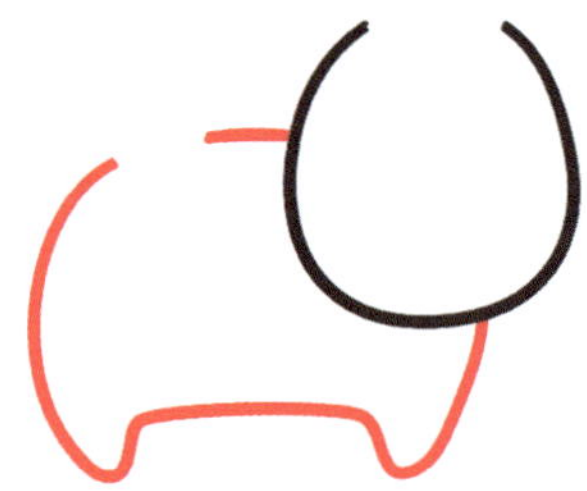

2. Draw a chubby body and legs. Leave a gap at the top for the wing.

3. Add a fluffy mane on top and a tail at the back.

4. Draw a front wing with some squiggles for detail. Then add a curved line for the back wing.

5. Finish the face by adding a snout, sparkly eyes, and tiny ears.

6. Color in your pegasus, using white to add sparkles on the wings, mane, and tail.

Centaur

1. Start with a slightly curved line for the chin, and then add a hairline to frame the face.

2. Draw the rest of the hair, leaving two gaps near the top for ears.

3. Add a small centaur body under the head.

4. Draw two big ears, two eyes, and a small mouth.

5. Add a tail, two arms, and a line at the waist.

6. Color in your centaur, adding some lighter-colored spots on the body.

Jackalope

1. Start by drawing a round head with a frill underneath.

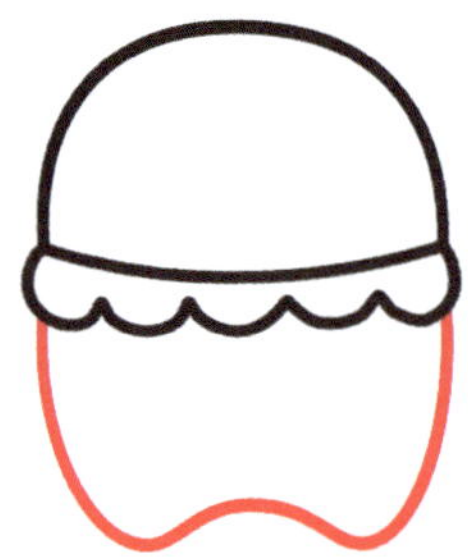

2. Add in the rest of the body.

3. Draw two eyes and a little nose.

4. Add two big ears and two little hands.

5. Draw two antlers on top of the head.

6. Color in your jackalope, using a lighter color for the tummy.

Unicorn

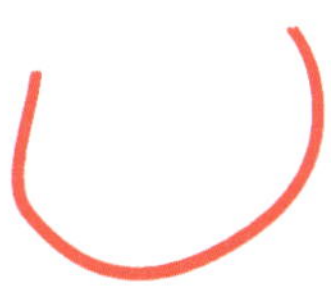

1. Start by drawing the head with a big gap at the top for the mane.

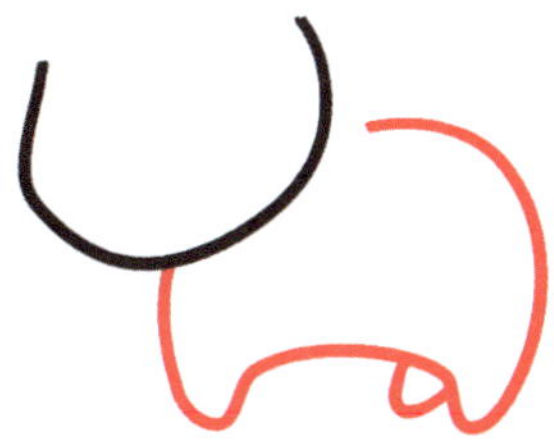

2. Draw the body and legs, leaving another gap near the head for the mane.

3. Add a horn above the head, and two curved lines for part of the mane.

4. Draw the rest of the mane and add a tail at the back.

5. Add the unicorn's ear, eye, nostrils, and mouth.

6. Color in your unicorn, adding some stars on the body and sparkles in the hair.

Amanita Mushroom

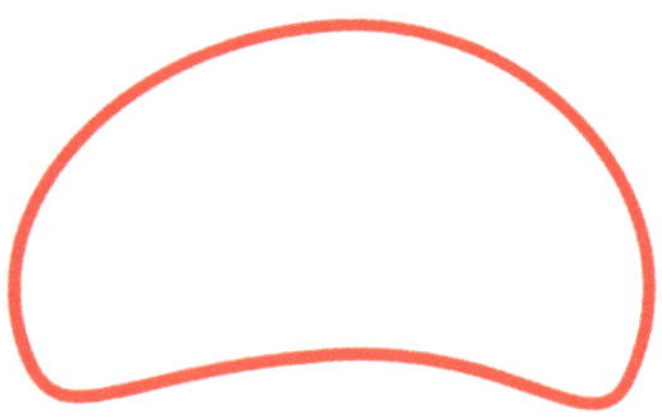

1. Start with a blob shape for the mushroom cap.

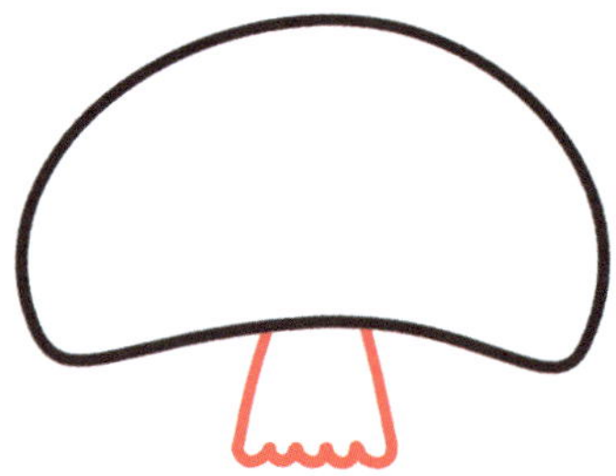

2. Draw a short stalk with a frilly bottom.

3. After drawing another frill, add the rest of the stalk with a rounded bottom.

4. Draw a curved line for the back edge of the mushroom.

5. Add some spots and a cute face.

6. Color in your mushroom.

Beech Mushrooms

1. Start with a small, squashed circle shape for the mushroom cap.

2. Add a long stalk with a wide rounded bottom.

3. Draw more small mushroom caps, randomly spaced around the first mushroom.

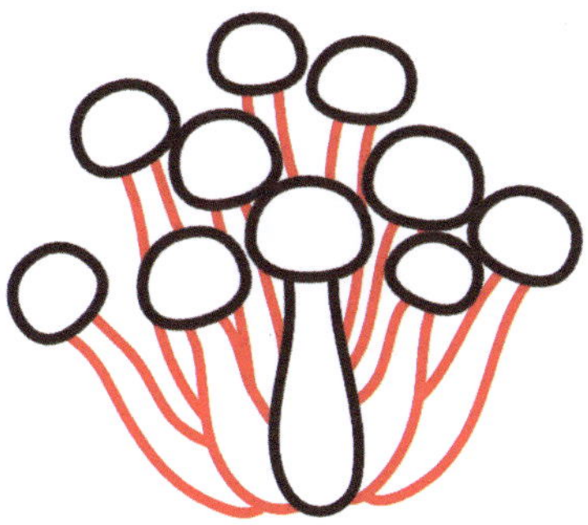

4. Give each mushroom a stalk, making them all meet together at the bottom.

5. Draw two little eyes on each mushroom cap.

6. Color in your mushrooms!

Bunch of Flowers

1. Start by drawing three small flowers with circles in the middle.

2. Draw some little tulips with small dots for eyes.

3. Add a few small circles in between the other flowers.

4. Draw a big bow underneath the flowers, leaving some space for the stems.

5. Add a stem to each flower, making the stems meet in the middle of the bow.

6. Add some pretty colors to your bunch of flowers.

Jade Plant

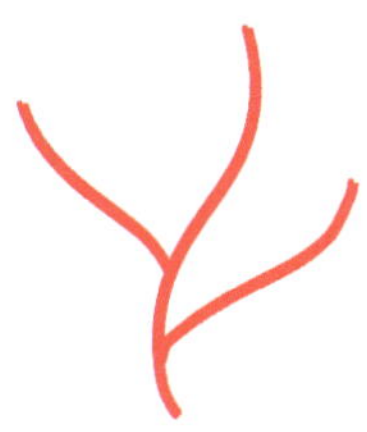

1. Start by drawing a main stem with two side stems.

2. Draw small, rounded leaves along each stem.

3. Add a squashed oval at the base of the main stem.

4. Draw the rest of the plant pot, and add a curved line near the top for the soil.

5. Give the plant pot two eyes and a mouth.

6. Color in your jade plant and plant pot!

Cactus

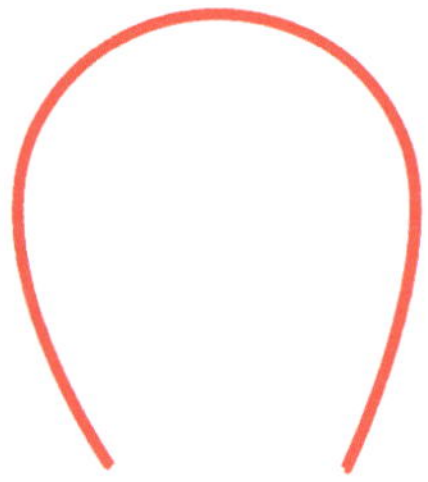

1. Start by drawing a big, curved line for the main part of the cactus.

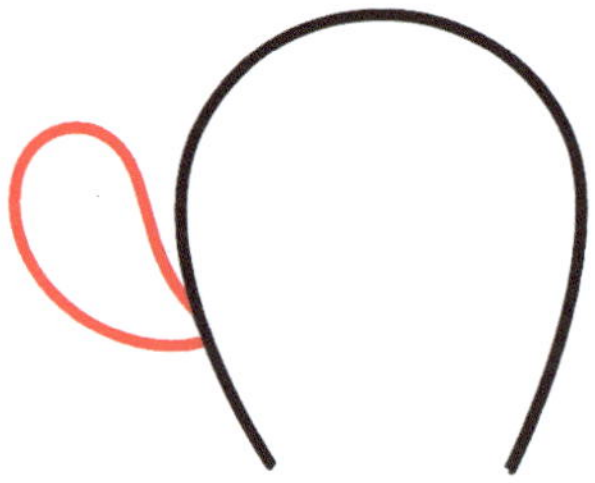

2. Draw a big arm on the side of the cactus.

3. Add a squashed oval shape for the top of the pot.

4. Draw in the rest of the pot, and add a curved line for the soil.

5. Give the cactus a face and some flowers on its head.

6. Color in your cactus, adding some white cross shapes for the spikes.

Bunny Succulent

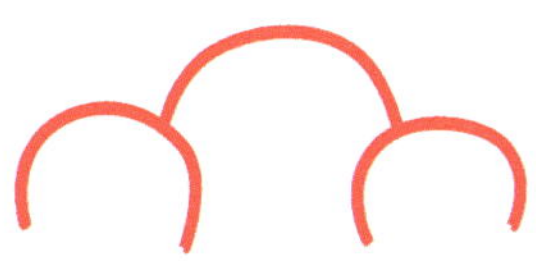

1. Start by drawing three little mounds.

2. Draw two long ears on top of each mound.

3. Add a squiggly line near the bottom of each mound.

4. Draw two curved lines for the plant pot.

5. Give each bunny two little eyes.

6. Color in your bunny succulent, decorating the pot with colored polka dots.

Pancake Plant

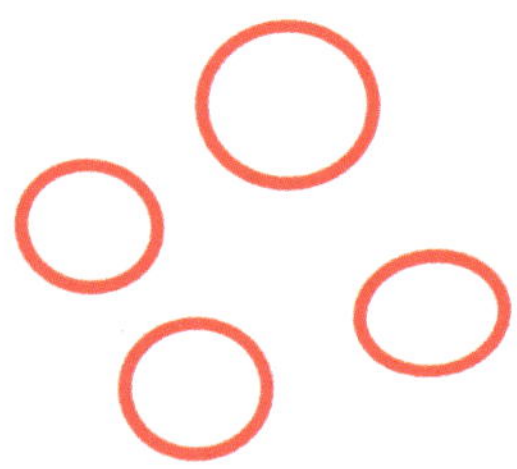

1. Start by drawing a few small circles and ovals for leaves.

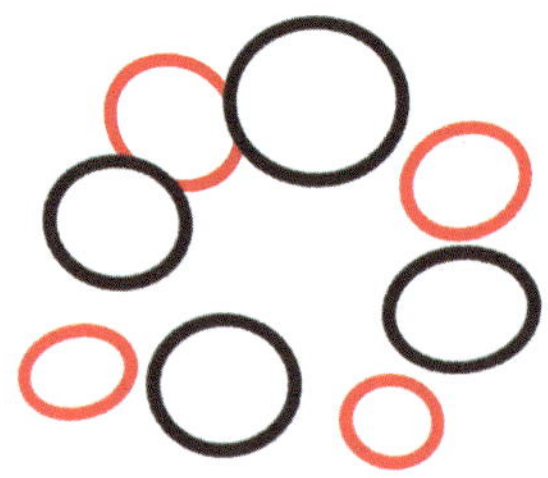

2. Add a few more leaves at different angles.

3. Draw a stem for each leaf, all joining in the middle.

4. Add a squashed oval shape for the top of the pot and a curved line for the rest of the pot.

5. Give the plant pot a cute face and add a curved line near the top for the soil.

6. Color in your pancake plant, adding pink ovals under the eyes for blush.

Snake Plant

1. Start by drawing three small, pointy leaves.

2. Draw some additional longer leaves behind the first three.

3. Add some more long, pointy leaves on top.

4. Draw a squashed oval for the top of the plant pot, and then draw the rest of the pot.

5. Add a line along the back edge for the soil, and give the plant pot a cute face.

6. Color in your snake plant. You can use different shades of green to add depth.

Spider

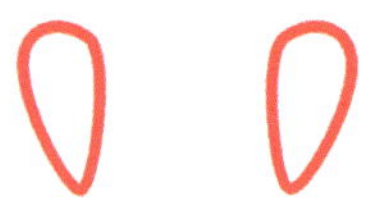

1. Start with two rounded triangle shapes for the front legs.

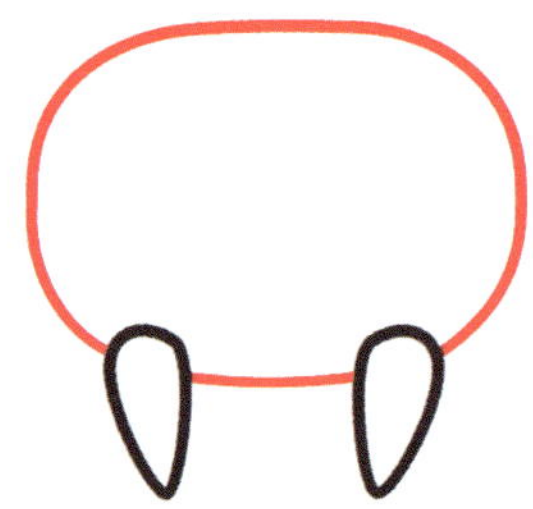

2. Draw an oval body just behind the two legs.

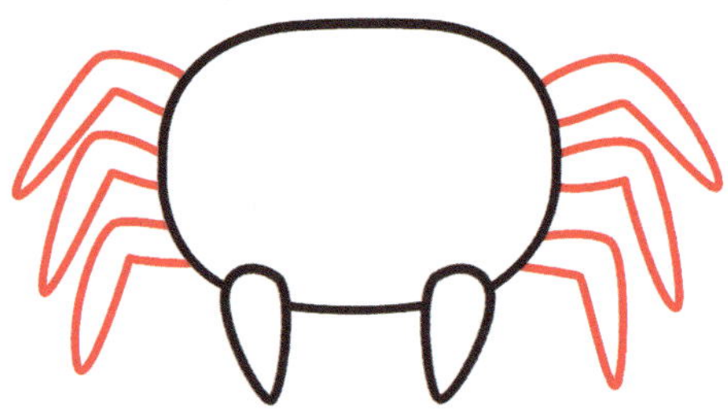

3. Add three more legs on each side of the body.

4. Draw two big eyes and a small mouth.

5. Add two more eyes on the sides of the head.

6. Color in your spider, adding pink blush on the face and stripes on the legs.

Dragonfly

1. Start by drawing a small oval shape for the body.

2. Add a long tail underneath the oval.

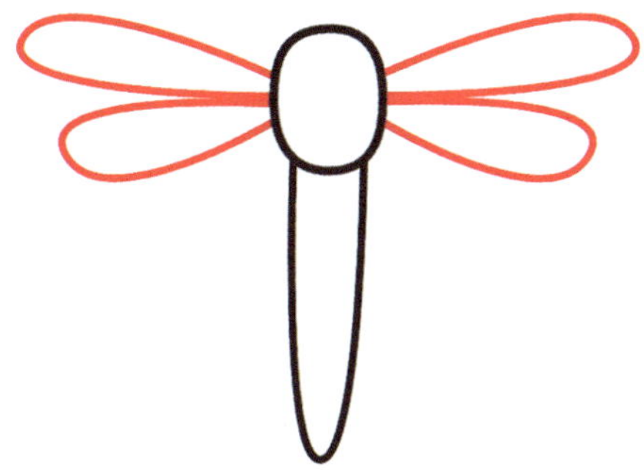

3. Draw two long, thin wings on each side of the body.

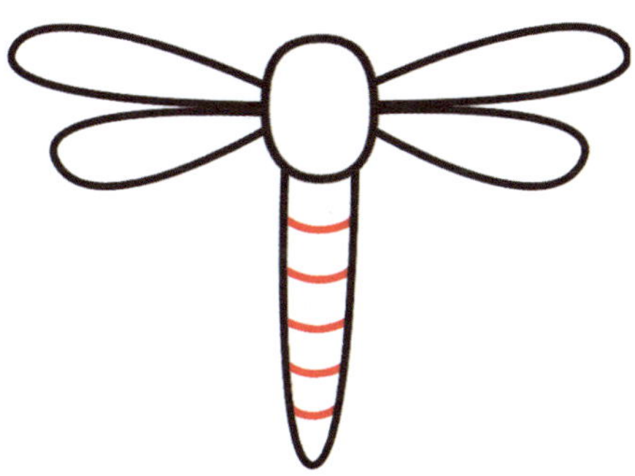

4. Add some curved lines for stripes on the tail.

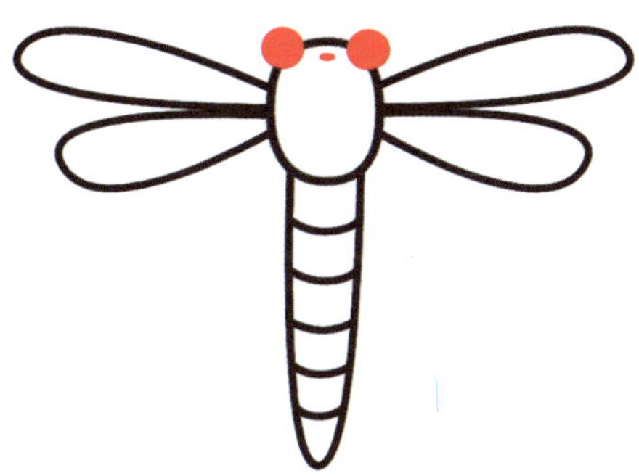

5. Draw two big eyes and a small mouth on top of the head.

6. Color in your dragonfly, using a light color for veins on the wings.

Ladybug

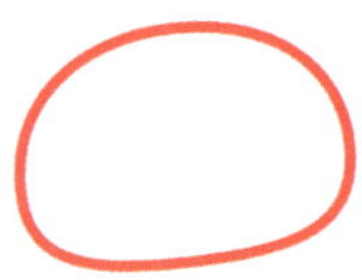

1. Start by drawing a blob shape for the head.

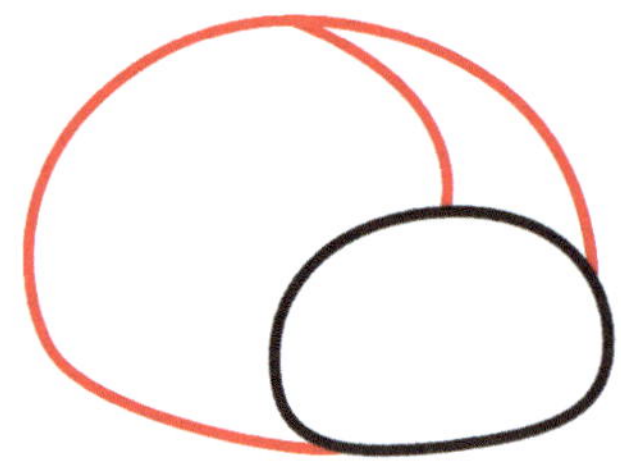

2. Draw a rounded loaf-shaped body behind the head. Add a line on the back where the wings meet.

3. Give the ladybug two feelers and some little lines for legs.

4. Draw some spots on the ladybug's body.

5. Add two big eyes and a small mouth.

6. Color in your ladybug.

Caterpillar

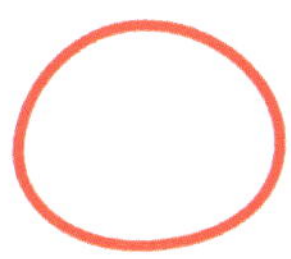

1. Start by drawing a slightly squashed circle for the head.

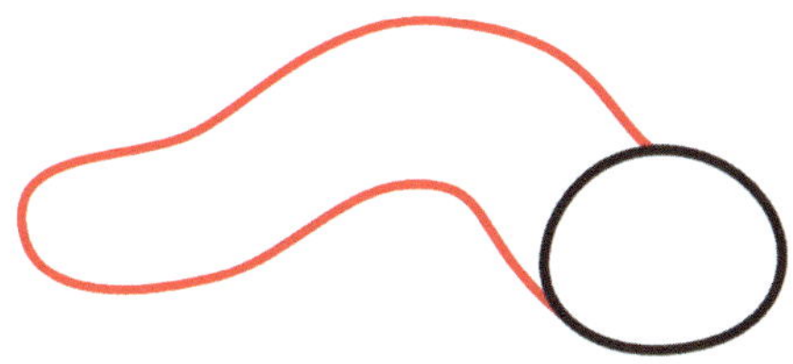

2. Draw the rest of the caterpillar's body, making it as long as you want.

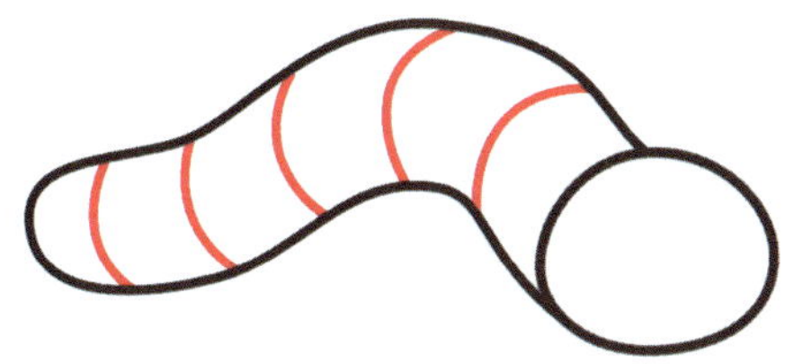

3. Add curved lines along the body for the segments.

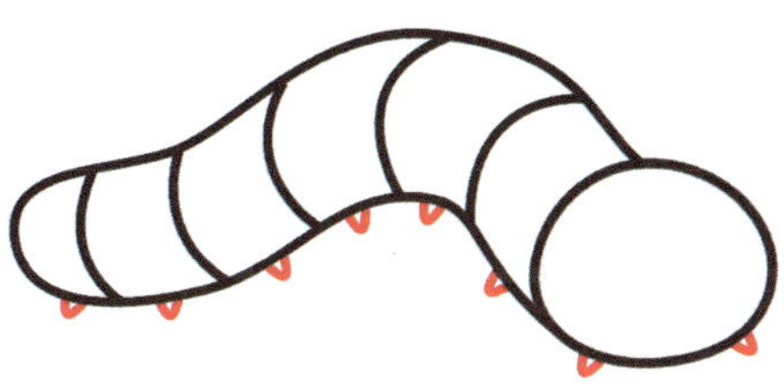

4. Draw some tiny feet along the bottom of the caterpillar.

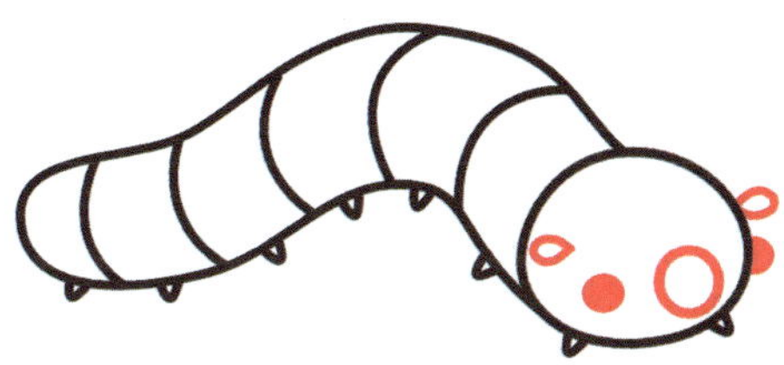

5. Add two eyes, a big open mouth, and two little feelers on the head.

6. Color in your caterpillar. You can use a different color for each segment to make it interesting!

Butterfly

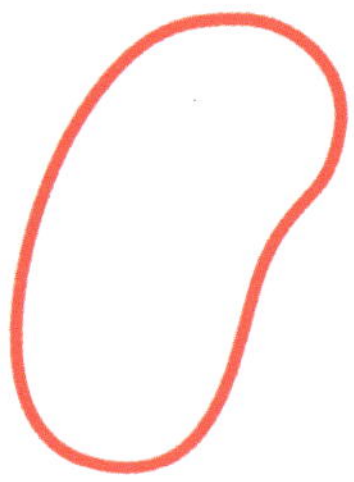

1. Start with a bean shape for the butterfly's body.

2. Draw a big wing on either side of the body.

3. Add some teardrop-shaped details onto the wings.

4. Give the butterfly two feelers and some stripes along the body.

5. Draw two eyes and a small mouth on the head.

6. Add whatever colors you'd like to your butterfly.

Snail

1. Start by drawing a spiral shape for the shell.

2. Add a big blob shape for the snail's body.

3. Draw two little feelers on top of the snail's head.

4. Add some polka dots onto the shell.

5. Give the snail two eyes and a small smile.

6. Color in your snail, adding light pink blush under the eyes.

Leaves

1. Start by drawing three curved lines for the leaf stems.

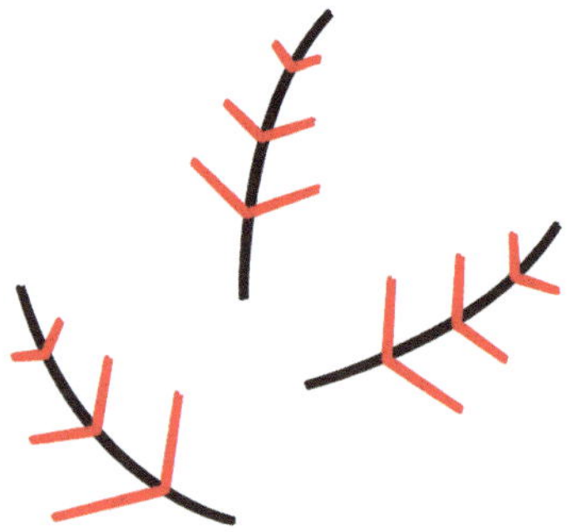

2. Add some angled lines for the leaf veins.

3. Draw a smooth leaf shape around one set of leaf veins.

4. For the second leaf, draw a squiggly line around the veins.

5. Draw some small leaf shapes around all the veins of the third leaf.

6. Use browns for autumn leaves or greens for a springtime feel.

Tiny Forest

1. Start by drawing three triangles with rounded corners.

2. Draw three more triangles behind the first ones.

3. Give each triangle a small rectangle for a trunk.

4. Add a squiggly line near the top of each tree.

5. Draw eyes on a few of the trees.

6. Color in your tiny forest, using white on the tops for snow.

Mountains

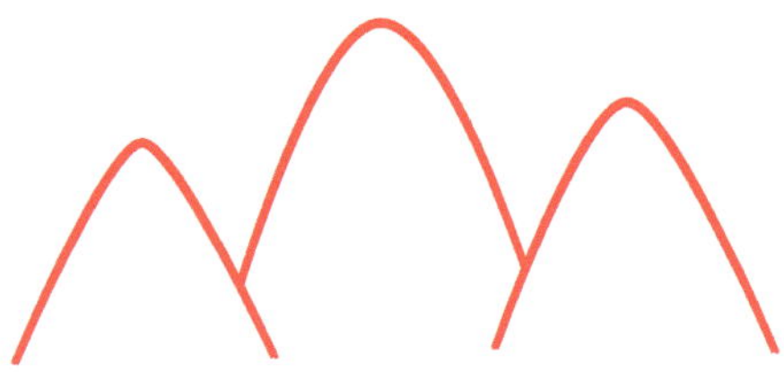

1. Start by drawing three open triangle shapes that overlap slightly.

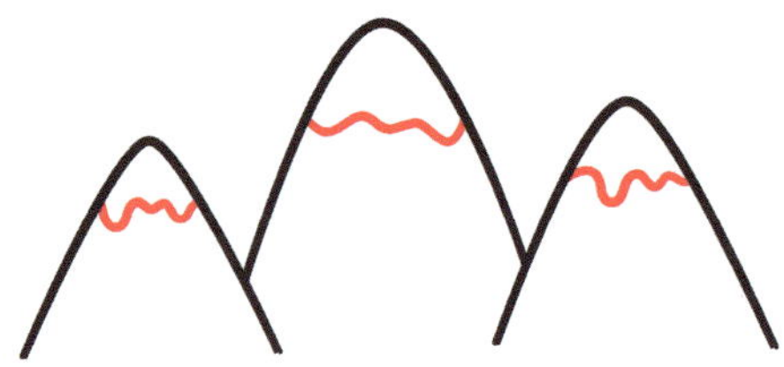

2. Draw a squiggly line near the top of each mountain.

3. Add a curved line at the base of the mountains.

4. Draw some fluffy clouds above the mountains.

5. Give each mountain a face. Try using different facial expressions!

6. Color in your mountains.

Shooting Star

1. Start by drawing a star shape with rounded corners.

2. Draw three long, curved lines on one side of the star for the trail.

3. Add some short, straight lines around the star.

4. Draw a few little sparkles around the trail.

5. Give the star a cute little face.

6. Color in your shooting star.

Rainbow & Clouds

1. Start by drawing a cloud shape.

2. Add another slightly smaller cloud shape next to the first one.

3. Draw two curved lines between the two clouds to create an arch shape.

4. Add five more curved lines inside the arch.

5. Give each cloud a cute face.

6. Use red, orange, yellow, green, blue, and purple for the rainbow colors. Then color the clouds with a light pink.

Moon & Stars

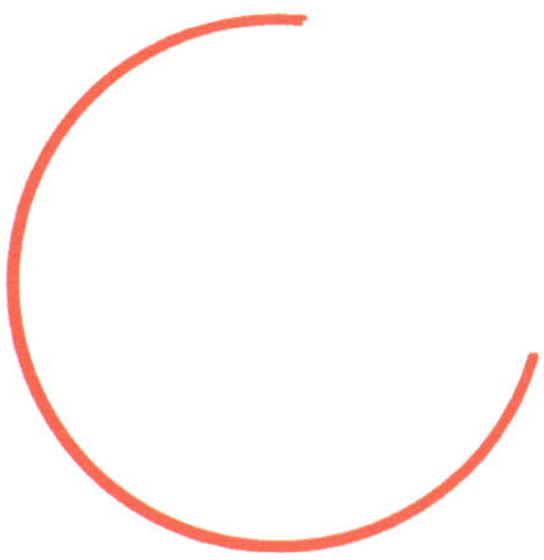

1. Start by drawing about two thirds of a circle.

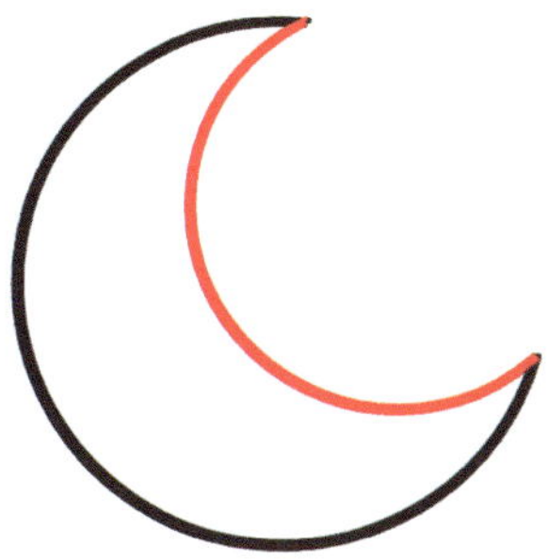

2. Draw a half-circle inside the first circle to form a crescent moon.

3. Add three little stars next to the moon.

4. Give the moon one sleepy eye and a small mouth.

5. Draw two little eyes on each star.

6. Color in your moon and stars, adding some darker spots on the moon for texture.

About the Author

Lauren Bergstrom was born and raised in South Africa and has been doodling cute things since she can remember. When she's not drawing or painting, she spends her time designing crochet patterns for little stuffed animals at mohumohu.com and making video games with her partner at Studio Any Percent. She lives in Canada with her family, in a small home filled with cute and fluffy things.